Advance Praise

Arlice W. Davenport's second work of poetry, *Everlasting*, is a literary gem, and Davenport, a poet of extraordinary talent and insight, subtly draws the reader into worlds of both mysticism and stark reality. Skilfully woven poetic devices give rise to phrases that appear to meld into one another seamlessly, colouring our minds and imagination with the beauty only a craftsman of his caliber can achieve.

Davenport's work is not merely intelligent but profoundly perceptive regarding the human condition, reflecting truths and thought-provoking ideas on many levels. His detailed descriptions and textural landscaping paint delicately honed imagery that is so beguiling one cannot be more transfixed by crafted language within such heartfelt expression.

The poet's offerings all feel deeply personal, as his authenticity and heart are so evident throughout, allowing his learned mind to delve into the recesses of verity and to nurture its blooming, gifted so warmly in every verse.

Descriptive works of nature, referenced classical mythology and history or worldly observations, each poem is interwoven like silk, shimmering threads of endless unfolding. Within these pages, across broad-spectrum humanity, are spotlit love, seasons, wonders, self-realizations, age, philosophy, spirit, experience and the recollections of a beautiful mind.
— **Tony DeLorger, award-winning author and poet**

After reading through *Everlasting* the first time, I turned back to the poem "Parting," which contains these words: "At first, the poetry would not hold...the words did not hold." My thoughts went of course, immediately to Yeats' "the centre cannot hold," thence to the thought that poetry and words are, indeed, at the center of it all, and then, finally, to this response: "Yes, Arlice," I murmured, "poetry and words are the center, but, my friend, as you demonstrate here in these pages, your poetry does hold; your words do hold."
— **Roy J. Beckemeyer, author of *Mouth Brimming Over***

Everlasting, by Arlice W. Davenport, is a series of books within a book. The first book opens with his poem "Stillness" and its expansive contrasting imagery. Davenport quickly sets a tone, with his reference to *askesis* and *apatheia*, that is without apology intellectual, and for this reader placed an inviting challenge to "keep up." The collection is unquestionably poetry, holding within its lines deeply emotive and expressive language using all the tools and literary devices one would hope for from a poet of this caliber.

He then digs into an overflowing and effervescent reservoir of knowledge of art history, the ancient world and its myths and legends, pulling that forward into the currency of now. What rises is a swell of Dali-like surreal imagery he uses to illustrate themes like inhumanity, alienation, conflict and sorrow. He chides indifferent and somnambulant attitudes toward pressing sociologic and environmental issues. In these poems you feel an angst and frustration that will be familiar. Davenport touches a raked nerve I, for one, have felt painfully pulsing within as he writes in "Morning Light," ". . . We fight alone, mired in the finite, craving the infinite."

The second book within his book delves into the existential and the divine. I loved reading "Ascendancy of Spirit." It is an excellent example of ekphrasis. In that poem Davenport uses Mark Rothko's color fields to explore defiant curiosity. In "Digging Deep," Davenport uncovers a sense of self that rises out of ". . . the agony of faith." In subsequent chapters he explores the fecundity of the human record and voices of other poets.

I am challenged to think of another book of poetry that offers the reader such an expanse of content and depth, reaching to the core of the human condition. This is a great read that I recommend with no hesitation.

— **Mark Andrew James Terry, editor** *Of Poets and Poetry*, **Vice President of the Florida State Poets Association (2021-22)**

In *Everlasting*, Arlice W. Davenport has taken up the universe in his open hand, reached toward eternity, grasped lightly the heavens and translated what he's seen to us mortals. In purity of language, the grit becomes polished, the dust breathes life, the film that covers sad eyes clarifies and turns into hope. A true dreamer, he speaks for many poets in that his words become magical and eternal.

— **Marilyn Griffin, retired librarian for the Corona / Norco Unified School District (CA), bookseller (Harvest Bookstore, Riverside, CA), and award-winning poet**

EVERLASTING

EVERLASTING

Poems by
Arlice W. Davenport

Meadowlark Press, LLC
Emporia, Kansas USA

Meadowlark Press, LLC
meadowlark-books.com
P.O. Box 333, Emporia, KS 66801

Everlasting: Poems
Copyright © Arlice W. Davenport, 2021

Cover Image: Public Domain. Credit: NASA, ESA, and the
Hubble Heritage Team (STScI/AURA),"Rose of Galaxies"
https://www.nasa.gov/mission_pages/hubble/science/hubble-
rose-gallery.html

Cover Design: Arlice W. Davenport and Laura J. Davenport

Interior Design: LG, Meadowlark Press

Author photo by a fellow traveler in Pompeii, Italy

POETRY / American / General
POETRY / Subjects & Themes / Places
POETRY / Subjects & Themes / General

ISBN: 978-1-7362232-7-7
Library of Congress Control Number: 2021940440

For Laura

She gazes at me,
and in the still light
of that impenetrable look . . .
the silence speaks!

I tremble in anticipation.

I listen and am fed.

– From "The Beloved"

Also by Arlice W. Davenport

Poetry:
Setting the Waves on Fire
(Meadowlark Press, 2020)

Poems

Book I
INTO THE MYSTIC

Book II
FINDING A SELF

Book III
PATTERNS OF FECUNDITY

Book IV
OTHER SHORES

EVERLASTING
Book I

INTO THE MYSTIC

Stillness

A great sky
opens within you,
speaks the rarefied
word of affection,
moves from this world
to the next, thrown down
like thunder, tuned up
like the tenor of dreams,
passing through
absence, presence,
askesis, apatheia,
the great uplift
of the desert,
the inundation
of the sea.

Light crests the cusp
of crumbled rocks.
Tranquility blinds
the inner eye.
It is a matter
of logic only,
this arid oasis,
this darkened cave.
You will climb
the barren tree
in stillness,
pluck harmony
from its branches,
hesitate,
perhaps meditate,
then repudiate
the Earth.

Deep Colors

The fiery ardor of the stars,
deep colors of existence.
Abandon the senses, rise
to the invisible through
the visible. Ecstatic love
draws out the underlying
layers that break through
the surface of things.

Take your palette and cake
impasto on your canvas.
Hidden figures emerge
from the refraction of red.
A prism of what will be
breaks apart into whites
and grays. Each day becomes
night, night becomes indigo.

Indigo metamorphoses
into a pale sky blue. Van Gogh
painted the last traces
of transcendence. What is seen
shivers, what is unseen circles
the sun. Behind that, a curtain
of black. Behind that, a curtain
of light where all senses cease.

Immersed in Desert, a Piece of Sky

1.
A moment in the morning,
and our minds are one.
We think the same thoughts,
desire the same desires,
will the same will.

2.
Neptune pulls himself up
from the sea, gaining
traction with his trident.
He controls the waves, yet they
hold him down like a captive crab.

3.
Light beaming flat through
the window. You cradle yourself
as if crying. No darkness looms,
only lovely, pure rays baptizing
your astonished eyes with joy.

4.
We rise to the other world
as jonquils rise through stones.
Will each petal resurrect, each
green stem? A bird distracts,
and the imagery blips away.

5.
Long lopes through the desert,
endless jaunts of monochromatic
loneliness. The soul feeds off

nothing, but must lean on something:
substance formed from the vital source.

6.
The blanket of night sprawls before us.
The quandary of burial. A piece of sky.
Soil rises to meet you. Everything
rises like the sweet smoke of incense.
Omnipresent, it beckons you to savor, then dream.

7.
An old man. A bowl of coins. He buys
nothing but time, which cannot be bought.
He buys new life, but it does not take cash.
Beg your way into heaven. A wedding feast
awaits. Immersed in desert, a piece of sky.

Unworldly

A white-hot orb gilds the naked trees,
singes the sky. Heat rises from the Earth,
dissipates through punctures in the ozone.
Those who disbelieve in global warming
feel sweat bathing their brow, eyes
stinging with salt. Nothing to do with our
polluted synergies, only Gaia's corrective.

My compass points neither here nor there.
Stars radiate light, ciphers of systems
of atoms whirling toward dark matter.
We wish upon them, then puzzle why
they dim and disappear. Distance deceives
us. It creeps closer than our breath. We
cannot measure it, immersed in ourselves.

True North exists only for those south, stuck
nearer the equator than the Antarctic Ocean.
Aurora Borealis beckons ever northward, but
the dancing hues are only Nature's watercolors,
running off paper into the depth of night.
It covers us with a dark blanket, comforting,
yet frightening. Our faults undisclosed, our

strengths unseen. The world is not our stage.
We strut upon it looking for *exit stage right*.
We thrive in artifice, our reflection the imprimatur
of the real. Stars, sun, the buckling Earth gather
no momentum in defining who we are, alienated
from the law of the wild, fixated on the destitution
of morality. War trumps famine, because

the starving die. Habitats no longer stand. Language
chokes on its own spittle. It cannot speak the absurdity
of the ideal. We pose as warriors of the good,
our conscience seared by untruth. We fight for freedom,
only to tie ourselves in knots of laws. We see
the whites of our own eyes. They are as porous as
the desert sand. We sift them into the unworldly.

Waves

1.
The solitary self seeks solace
away from the anonymous *they*.
An ordinary summer evening,
humid and warm. Cicadas chatter.
Dusk creeps ever westward.
Blackened trees quiver in the breeze.
The Earth digs its own grave
in the dark, lingers on strips
of just-planted sod. No current
sweeps the dead underground, which
precedes, succeeds all inhabitants.

2.
Blue-green waves wriggle toward
the gulls. Basalt pyramids litter
the beach. The sun gilds the thin
horizon, paints pink, low-hanging
clouds. Color spells opulence,
an embarrassment of riches.
Who would steal them belongs
to the backwater *they*, who
long to see in black-and-white,
to choose an identity of
innocuous gray. Moths burn.

3.
Light illumines, obscures the ground
of Being. Descent mimics ascent:
pure movement toward the beyond.
Clarity rings the gong of recognition.
Know thyself. Yes, but which self
knows, which is known? *They*:

There is only one mind, practical,
hard-working, seeking comfort
from corruption. Crabs feed
on flotsam. Sandy footsteps
vanish in errant waves.

Parting

At first, the poetry would not hold,
invisible, weightless, clinging
to the tendrils of sorrow.

No light could enter your
writer's cave. No life, no dawn,
no joy at the simple act of being.

I called your name, only the stillest
voices answered, only the wine stain
on the table, only the errant wish.

We walk, somnambulant, through
life, you said, startled by birds
in trees, waking to the vision

of mercy, wrapped in a mandala
of orange and blue, rising to peaks
of broken urns, dulled cobblestones.

In Umbria, you filled the winding
lanes with love, landscapes
serenaded your muted passion.

Elongated cedars cast shadows
on the undulant green lawn. Tickets
south fluttered in the wind. No passage.

Only connect. Yet the words did not hold.
I see you in Assisi, PAX carved into
the eternal shrubbery. You laughed

at Giotto's cartoons, took notes on
St. Francis' prayers. Italy weightless,
invisible, clinging to your nameless sorrow.

Orvieto

1.
Below the towering facade
of the cathedral, you rummage
through a cache of signs: Humility
feeds the pilgrims' progress.

Even the mammoth, Gothic columns
ignite. Into the *Piazza del Duomo*,
gladiolas breathe, sweet scent
of the dead spared desecration.

2.
The urge to rise, to transcend, to blossom
into wings, to scale ladders, to build altars
in the scalding magma of the Holy.
Time is no more the enemy than God.

Freed from the Signorelli frescoes
in San Brizio Chapel, Satan primps like
a Dostoyevskian dandy. Low currents
of your voice, the melancholy of Christ.

3.
We live by longing, a vocation of desire
that circles the crypt. What is left but
the mystery of the underworld, the overworld,
the village fountains flowing with light?

Beauty resides beyond Being, a drunken
star, an extravagant river that flows
through the nave into the hills. No word
about the desert, dust or ash. Only *la vita nuova*.

Everlasting

I slog through brackish waters. Your
voice winnows on the wind, each
word plucked from an eagle's plumage,
each quill elliptical and tattooed,
each hieroglyph bleached clean by the sun.

Love buries the future deep within
its manicured strata of sod, hedges
trimmed as Greek pillars, soft edges
peeling away green foliage, until
only Aphrodite's ruined temple remains.

Time foists on us no favors, the present
hanging midair like a hummingbird
skittish to flit into the past, suckled
by nectar of bell-shaped flowers,
spilling beveled raindrops on the earth.

Runes rise above the firmament, chiseled
teeth without food. Immune to sacred
mysteries, immersed in ancient history, they
seed the everlasting. Frayed feathers settle
on berms. Brackish waters cleanse the sky.

Spring

Summer's promise
pools at the edge
of the snow,
a white medallion
gliding on
dull grasses.
Saucer-sized puddles
bathe the earth,
splashing pebbles
and spatters
of mud. I plant
a precision-cut
boot print next
to a budding
crocus. A burst
of orange
beams from
the blackened soil.

In my neighbor's
field, a bobcat
scurries past
for sheer pleasure.
Its satellite
ears turn
in every direction,
detecting my
wayward steps.
I keep my distance,
but marvel
at the cat's
movement
away from,

then toward
the yellowed
hedge row.

I roam,
backward
and forward,
beside the ragged
bank of snow,
kneel in
the oozing mud,
write my new name
at the beckoning
of Spring.

Pastoral

The road rises silently in the wind.
Twin yellow tracks push past
the green pasture's edge, infinitely
curving into the soft face of the woods.

Trees bristle like the wayward wool
of freshly sheared sheep,
naked to the sun's burning touch
on their pliant, pink flesh.

There is no turning back from
the white evening glare, no
route to rouse a heightened
sense of romance or joy.

A dark cry of geese burbles above
the pond. They flap frantically
to outrun the weight of the world,
forever gaining on their flight.

I bark back, only to marvel as they
levitate higher, wings beating
like a common pulse, beaks pointed
homeward, then dive-bombing to safety.

In the ancient sky, the sun bleeds orange-red.
V-shaped shadows scour my path.
I could take the road less traveled,
but there is only one road, rising

silently in the western wind. To walk
it now, alone, makes no difference.

Morning Light

1.
The waning voice of the hills means
no great loss. Tepid pools collect dew,
spew mist into the morning miasma
of the new, of dawn's breaking on
the reddened horizon, riddling bracken
and heather with dappled rays of gold.

Within this fevered world of promise,
I struggle to find a lasting path forward.
No whispering wind points the way,
no guide awaits, adorned in shadow.
Each step shall be my first and my last,
forging a sacred road through
the fractured landscape. Birds flutter
in my wake, flummoxed by invasive noise.

Clouds tie the nascent sky in knots, pull
taut the strings of cirrus streaking through
the hemisphere of blue, too early for their cue,
too thin to bless the earth with rain. They lack
the muscle of thunderheads, which pummel
dust into mud, impregnate sun-drunk flowers
with sodden pollen, pistils limp, petals
shaped into bell-like goblets to catch the flow.

2.
I have left behind a lifetime of riches, buried
in the past, obliterated into oblivion, hidden
underground with the dead, who count
wealth in opportunities missed: windows
to re-create the possibility of victory with
the simple toss of the dice, with the winning card

tucked safely away in your hand. I am no gambler,
but I thrill to the endless chase for glory.

Everything depends on its radiant flux. How it
enlarges the self, how it rises above the mundane,
sharing in the grandeur of the gods, who frolic
in the lowly human's plight. Our heroes began
as flesh and blood: Hercules, Achilles, Odysseus.

Who will call on them to savor our triumphs?
Who will fly to our aid when Apollo turns his back?
None can say nor dare invoke the Delphic Oracle.
We fight alone, mired in the finite, craving the infinite.
O mercy without end. When will you come? When
will we die in the edict of the eternal: the present
everlasting, now wholly human?

The Heart of Riddled Memory

The winnowing sun
glints off the quay
only to be swallowed up
in shadows. The pillar
beneath the bridge proffers
cover from the rain, as names
swirl out of the mists
into the empty chambers
of my brain. Names: familiar
yet I have forgotten them
like the brush of some
stranger rushing near
on a winter's night.
How I would recapture
the past if only the shadows
consumed time, if only the names
meant someone I could reach.
Only uncertainty is real,
only the wariness of pain
permeates my days.
Shall I saunter along
the quay, crossing the bridge
in search of light, in search
of lost time like Proust in his
cork-lined room? The mists
sink into the Seine. I must
follow them to the end as
the river empties into the Channel
at Le Havre. In the distance
ships bellow through the dark,
calling me to surrender
to the heart of riddled memory:
to remember only what
returns, always the same,
yet ever changed by the night.

Open Fields

(After Camus)

Stones steam,
slowly sink
into the earth,
reclaim origins,
grooming,
grinding
the ground
of Being,
as ruins of time
recapitulate
their rococo facade.

I try in vain to match
my breathing
to the world's
tumultuous stammer.
Wave upon wave
of wind surges
through gashes
in the arid soil,
where nothing
grows but ennui.

Nothing stirs
but pebbles,
searching for
their halcyon days
as cornerstones,
foundations
of civilizations'
grand edifices,
great walls built
to hold back death.

We watch the reaper
pulse his way
into open fields,
unfit to fathom
the seeds of
germination.
We grant him
passage under
the sun's thin film,
somnambulant,
insensate, sturdy
as a stack of stones.

ℰVERLASTING
Book II

FINDING A SELF

The Philosopher Rises

1.
ahead of all parting
looms the loss of beginning
the tentative way forward to a sorrowful ending

what is   is not   yet remains the same
contraries sublimate silently
in the shadow of philosophy

chaos breeds nostalgia for the unity of desire
disunity divides   erects barriers
of vast conundrums of being

2.
humans spring up to question all
even their need to question all
even their urge to answer none

Thales fell into a well contemplating
the underlying stuff of the universe
he named it water   others said air   earth   fire

3.
philosophy is born   Socrates stars as midwife
drawing out fledgling lovers of wisdom
almost all return to Athens' life of power and lies

Socrates drank hemlock in a prone position
relaxing against an imaginary couch
flat on cold stone his legs turned frigid and blue

4.
the gods are One   their diversity yields
only a failure of divinity   their foibles perch
at the falling-off point of justice and mercy
Zeus seduces as a swan   mates with mortals
spawns offspring merely human in form
his virtue fails before the intensity of lust

death hides like a hedgehog in a badger's den
jaws snap the bumpy surface of the spine
thus the philosopher rises beyond good and evil

The Inertia of Desire

Perhaps it is the dusty balustrade, leading,
    unbidden, to the upper stories.
Perhaps the insignificance of choice.

Perhaps it is the spindly daffodil, yellow trumpet
    turned toward rain.
Perhaps the weariness of work tied only
    to tomorrow.

Perhaps it is the high ceilings of the rooms
    empty of memory.
Perhaps the misery that spurs life to spring
    into light.

Perhaps it is the infinite repetition of
    the quotidian.
Perhaps the steep gravel lane descending
    from the woods.

Perhaps it is the vine on the trellis choked
    by unwitting weeds.
Perhaps the Edenic garden of earthly delights.

Perhaps it is the sprig of white heather,
    token of his love.
Perhaps the tears of his betrothed, staring
    down the void.

Perhaps it is the coolness of the brow pressed
    against marble slabs.
Perhaps the glory of the Greeks, preserved
    in their hubris.

Perhaps it is the tragedy of freedom, wrecked
    upon harbor rocks.
Perhaps the delicate touch of comfort after
    the anguish of death.

Perhaps it is the future creeping up
    on the restlessness of time.
Perhaps the eternal moment overlooked
    by blinkered historians.

Perhaps it is the poet's task, freed from linguistic
    stricture.
Perhaps the divine imperative to speak, but never
    die.

Perhaps it is the wonder of possibility, shorn
    of necessity.
Perhaps the hollowness of thought pushed
    past the limits of the word.

Perhaps it is the beckoning of art to salvage
    the self-conscious few.
Perhaps the immortality of the self, rooted
    in Being.

Perhaps it is the seaweed on the shore, viscous
    and oozing.
Perhaps the sand in your shoes, grinding
    at your feet.

Perhaps it is the ruse of destruction, claiming
    to make all things new.
Perhaps the end of *agonistes*, the solace
    of the wise.

The Future

1.
An island rises
in the morning mist,
uninhabited by all
but the most
frenetic birds.

It is the future
coming toward me,
isolated and green,
the shore splayed
with tumbled stone.

Ancient trees
bend at the waist
of gargantuan trunks.
I take root in
the Encompassing.

2.
Shells litter the sand
as the tide recedes.
Winds roil the sky.
All paths turn inward.

I plunge into time,
grasp the fading now.
Waves cover my past,
wash the coming light.

Trees sway in the wind.
Schools of fish rise.
Days lean in delight.
The future angles back.

Ascendancy of Spirit

1.

I crawl across the shimmering fault lines
that wall off Rothko's color fields, blithely
skimming the edges, feathered toward eternity,
deftly darting across the hairline abyss
that wavers from orange to yellow and back again.
No map charts this territory, self-referential, self-
renewing, self-examined until the paints dry up
and the artist's hand aches from ascetic excess.

2.

Saturated in soulful hues, I balance like a ballet
dancer, *en pointe*, at the core of each irregular
rectangle, brushing up against divisions in
the color wheel that whirl around the expressionist
palette, united only by the suicidal willfulness of a man
who has exhausted all callings, resisting the urge
to paint only black, caving in on itself, carving out
the brush's final resting place, soul within soul.

3.

Rothko contains millions. He breathes
life into the inchoate cosmos, even as
he seduces death. He siphons The Big Bang
into transcendental planes of primal hues
haloed by an absence so intense it bursts
into presence. We find no streams
of consciousness seeping through his canvases,
only an ascendancy of spirit into the dying void.

To-Do List

To sift the seeds of ruin
beneath an ancient sun.
To breathe the warmth of rain
that melts the mounded snow.
To count the loss of time
with echoes faint and still.
To woo a guarded love
under a cynic's sky.
To comfort the aggrieved
with weary words of pain.
To write an epic poem
without meter or rhyme.
To boost my sense of joy,
then play a losing hand.
To dwell in inwardness
while others stone my soul.
To ask for nothing real,
but linger in despair.
To trim the cacti's spines,
and let the clippers sag.
To praise the feudal reign
while dying as a serf.
To say, "All seek for thee"
in vast, vacant deserts.
To lift the builder's crane
with opposable thumbs.
To turn Rothko's works back
to figurative art.
To see angles at night:
Euclid behind the eye.
To call out in distress,
then settle for handshakes.
To embrace the absurd,

ignore Camus' *The Rebel*.
To pray that art can save,
only to watch words die.
To champion drama,
as the curtain crumples.
To take a final bow,
blinded by the footlights.

Love Immemorial

The poverty of memory blanches
all objects of desire. Events gurgle up
from an unconscious soup, evanescent
as bubbles in a fine champagne,
diligent as cells churning blood into oxygen.
I recall our clinging fast to each other,
the first kiss an interlocking piece
of the sexual puzzle that forever lacks
the solution's final fragment.

Love plays with matches
in the winter wind. Remembrance
whisks past, pressed to avoid
the cost of recreating what is only
ghostly, of swinging on naked branches
to materialize as mind. O how the past
sucks the marrow from our bones,
leaving limp limbs, parallel thumbs.
How we yearn for substance,
for a love immemorial, a lasting
kiss sans mound or stone.

Digging Deep

I have dirtied my hands
with the agony of faith.
Digging deep to find commitment,
smoothing soil to hide despair,
heaping mounds of stone
as facsimiles of evidence.

Add water, and dirt turns malleable.
I squeeze a human body out of the dark clay,
breathe life into it,
then write my name in the residue.
Mud covers all but the letter "A."

Supplication

A melody falls from cloud
to stone. A god sings and
splits the fallow ground.
Each note turns blue beside
the rusted plough. Hollow
men throw seed into
blackened rows. Blackened
wheat spirals to the azure sky.
Orpheus and his lyre summon
the uneasy dead. Love climbs
twisted vines. Great ruddy grapes
spill into jars of wine:
ambrosia of the gods.

Who encroaches on silence
defiles his destiny. Who scales
high walls spies Elysium.
Music echoes from isle
to isle, lodging in blue-gray
waves. The lyre sounds from
the sky beyond the sky.
Salt extinguishes fire. Songs
clip the wings of sea-weary
vessels. No tide will bring back
Eurydice or the moon
or the wallowing wails of the dead.
Retrieve the melody from cloud,
unite its voices in blackened
harmony. Supplicate for more.

Ego

There is nothing left
when the snows swirl,
the wizened apple falls,
the hills turn tawny
and dry. I twist in search
of the cirrus-shredded
sky. Hawks soar,
return to land,
swoop away again,
carrying my ego
in their hypodermic
talons, now heavy
with wounded prey.

My Name

orange dragon clouds
swirl in the dusky, baroque, winnowing sky
the once brilliant day dies within me
i cling to a rocky pinnacle   alone
one more step and i will laugh
my way toward heaven and
count the teeth of mountains
empty space my only confidante
crooked lines my only name

Heritage

We whittle away the day
into shavings of cedar.
Behind us, vineyards claw
the hill. Before us, the sea
crashes into stone. The Ligurian
coast curls past the horizon,
headed north toward Levanto.

Italy charms us like a magician
making flowers appear.
We pluck the petals,
lavender and pink, soft hues
to welcome the sunset splaying
below the clouds like the under-
wash of watercolors steeped

in delicate pastels. Here, simplicity
embraces beauty like a vine
entwines a tree. The symbiosis
runs slowly, subtly, expressing
the will to power, the *élan vital*.
We unite in the force of love
for each other, for the world,

for the heart of Cinque Terre,
for the vast Italian past. A heritage
of spirit and might, upholding
the sweetness of cedarwood,
the enduring substance of stone.
We walk the *Via dell'amor*, slipping
on the damp trail. Ahead, gulls serenade
our way as the blackened sea sweeps
our path, our love surging home.

— For Laura

EVERLASTING
Book III

PATTERNS OF
FECUNDITY

More

Strange the stages of breathlessness.
More and more, there is less and less.
The final pump of a ventilator
and less is liberated, unknowingly, into more.

Half a face, out of focus, staring into nothingness,
pained and lost. More and more, loss is less and less:
the human touch surgically removed. Less is never
more until the face of death slithers into focus.

Schubert's string quartets play through my head.
More is more is more. Less is the worm in the heart
of Being: only a vapid caesura fringed by vibrations
of sweetness and power. More bows down to more.

Mending Wall

Green glistens along the landscape,
interrupted by patches of yellow
and tan, great blocks of black
bordered by straight, imaginary lines—
the rigid signature of ownership.

At dusk, I have seen screech owls flee
their trees on a hurried hunt for prey.
They do not spy divisions in their gestalt,
only grey fur, drowsing before dinner,
unaware of descending talons, or the beak
soon tearing flesh into ragged strips of red.

Frost's mending wall has crumpled into dust,
apples and cows mingling freely, like ants,
but no workers stir among them. *Good fences*
make good neighbors now built on cliché
rather than hand-hefted stone, or good-natured
détente in the face of an uneven, burdensome
barrier. The land laps up the dust, laughs just the same.

Creation

Let there be a harbor, a castle, a tumultuous sea.
Let there be gulls that shed their feathers for outfits of blue.
Let there be orange eyes on the tower's medieval clock face.
Let there be dead leaves blowing through the corner café.
Let there be cheese-braided rope to hold tugs at bay.
Let there be nets for drowned sailors, plump with silver and coal.
Let there be fish who ogle Venus on the sun-washed half-shell.
Let there be locks of hair blooming like seaweed in the canal.
Let there be cannons firing legions of purple saints.
Let there be clouds that slice through the day's freshly baked
    bread.
Let there be poets who feast on the bones of their elders.
Let there be peace in the shroud of a wounded world.
Let there be light on the mountains in the shape of love.
Let there be Being, Becoming, then holding down Nothing.
Let there be hope in the architecture of Plato's cave.
Let there be truth forcing wars toward blood-soaked ground.
Let there be pins that stitch trust to the undergarment of time.
Let there be a Renaissance of invention for the jingling keys
    of life.

Unfinished Dialogue

"Our wisdom is the wisdom of the
desert," she said, "of dry, empty places,
of lethargy and longing, of renunciation and flight."

I watched her walk into the blurry heat waves
of the horizon, her carriage erect,
arms raised like a saguaro cactus, prickly as a porcupine.

She had no means of rescue, no parting from
her environs, her faded countenance scrubbed
clean by endless sand. "Mediocrity will be our

downfall," she cried as she splayed a cobalt blue onto
the dome above, spattered it with white, an orange
peel for a moon, coyote's howl as serenade.

"We long for fullness, completion, the hidden way
of happiness. Yet we cannot admit our misery. We
cannot admit the weakness that makes

us dream of oases, water gushing from stones,
the evening primrose." Such hyperbole, I thought,
so many wounded birds, so many buried serpents,

the vision of unreason, the defiance of hope.
How can we see ourselves clearly with this sty
of helplessness in both eyes, with no radiating sun?

She never looked back, advancing on the night,
gazing up at the heavens, sensing no wisdom from
above, alone with her silent witness of the dunes.

Fire

Do we not sense the pattern of a leaf in flight?
Its elliptical descent into grasses and shrubs.
Its affinity for sidewalks. We burn leaves
as an autumn ritual. Fire cleanses, cauterizes,
brands the bloom of summer on our minds.

Do we not know the pain of unrequited love?
The persistent desire. The ache of alienation.
The hopelessness and death. We burn loves
as a human ritual. Fire scorches, scars,
brands a gallows on our heart.

Do we not yearn for infinite possibilities?
The transcendence of existence. The grasp
of Being, timeless and new. We burn selves
as an existential ritual. Fire reshapes, rehearses
our yearnings, brands a circle on our loss.

The Temptation of St. Anthony

1.
another mortal cul de sac
   the Egyptian desert
luxe, calme et volupté
phantasmagoria of the fasting
soul   Flaubert's alter ego
for thirty years
                ascetic prose
      obsessive precision
                the Norman revises each word
for *lust, assault, desire*
      each phrase morphs
into a naked temptress
      demons demand allegiance
to the heraldry of heresy
      monsters extend their hands
            caress with a sensual touch
                        Anthony dies to himself
half-rises   and dies again

2.
gold pressed into giant *fleurs de lis*
hovers over outstretched trees
that pirouette toward what shines
      brightest
                the saint   illiterate
      ill-fed   weaving webs of Scripture
in his head   wielding prayers
as shields of Attic bronze   against
the blasphemous
                battery of spirit
strength matches strength
      solitude yields sanctity   strife
of manhood and mission   Eros
buries in repression
sublimation breeds beatification

3.
all roads lead to Plato's cave
   shadows shun substance
   consume fading fires
             Anthony wraps
his names in light   crosses out darkness
with bits of charcoal   feeds phantoms   to the pit
   kingdom of the sun illumines all souls
   conquers cupidity   dons prayer scroll
of initiation
        finds bondage of the will

resistance means intentionally
          letting be
   baptize the fight
   evil rises like heat
   blue flames turn
white   blanch canyon walls   shadows
cast spells   tumble to the desert floor
        dust settles on Anthony's wounds
        demon bones litter the hills

Thirst

The angle of repose
bruises the sun
with splotches
of blue. An invisible
hand imprints circles
of fire on my neck.
I drink from shallows
in shadow. They taste
muddy, dank and warm.
On the breeze, a scent
of lilac lingers. I must change
my path to imbibe her solace.

Honey

Irises droop under
the weight of glory,
elongated petals like pristine
evening gloves, buttoned-up,
tight-fitting, tanned before
dyeing. Bees huddle midair,
hunting nectar from the blooms.
Beauty, tasteless, cannot
be curried into combs
of honey. It resists all force.

I hear flitting wings flatten
in the wind. The sound
of failure, sweet nothings
breathed against the arid sky,
which croons blues, a ballad
of heartbreak, of glory
defiled. I thirst for rain,
for the issue of fonts
splashing beads of life.
I recount them as I drink.

Dust storms scour
the mournful moon,
craters fill, faces
scrubbed into anonymity:
the substance of chalk.
Come too near, and tides
pummel the shore. Too far,
waves recede in solitude,
in search of shelter, invisibility,
the buzzing of bees.

Can we live outside ourselves,
stand next to who we are?

I reach for my silver mask,
force my lips into a grimace.
Smiling seems so banal when
others' sorrow sweeps past.
I could ride this surge until
only foam trickles on sand.
A fleeting beauty unknown to bees,
tasteless as sterile honeycombs.

Red, Black, Fire

A scarlet slash
across a fresco-free wall.
Fire, desire, blood, love.
A pimply stone surface
invites irregularity,
the unevenness of breath.

Exhale the forms
that do not fit your frame.
Inhale the rule of thirds,
perspective's vanishing point.
All architecture ends
in an omnivorous black hole.

Black holes intimate
what once was. Light,
form, energy, fire. Rays
of naught bathe what is,
gravity's gravitas. Even
tragedy will not endure.

A scarlet sash
encircles a waist, the map
of self-overcoming, the hillock
of consummation, the valley
pulsing with rain. *Paint it
black* mitigates nothing.

Villages renew themselves
in the hidden glow of comets.
A marriage flutters the sky
in white, hue of purity
and Being. The sun blanches
all traces of red, settles for green.

Scarlet transmutes into
fragments of prisms.
Fire, desire, blood, death.

The Long, Green Grass

We laid out in the long green grass
And never thought that it would pass
    —Van Morrison, "A County Fair"

sharpened blades of grass
slice through evening shadows
which fragment like a cubist portrait

our legs point toward the rising brook
water gurgles over pebbles
streams into the dale
climbs the hillside
settles in a pool of diamond dragonflies

their optical wings magnify
the countryside's pure pleasures
unrepeatable cycles of new forms
new trees new hillocks
new havens for pilgrims

O how we lay in the morning dew
alone save for fidgety rabbits
who flicked by our sleepy heads
eyes closed to all but the spectacle within

where streams flow into themselves
where the sun circles a field of daisies
turning heads toward the southwestern sky
planting kernels in bare patches of soil

we have come late to our own renewal
to rejoining our source with full force
with fluid identities
with constant bleary eyes

when we lay together that year stars spilled
across our torsos like a vein in the marble
of Rilke's fractured sculpture of Apollo
you must change your life of course

a true poem grows in a field of sharpened grass
surges toward the brook
until it becomes the blade
reflecting our fragmented faces

Adagio

Samuel Barber's "Adagio for Strings"
floats through the open door.
Hummingbirds preen on nectar
outside the picture window.

In the movement of their wings,
in the movement of the strings:
the somber tone of death,
the infinity into which we die.

A clear high note reverberates
from the violin, reaching
the celestial spheres,
which extend ever outward

toward that which resonates
within us, *like attracted to like*,
the mystic chord of harmony,
of melody, of meaning in moans.

I listen and weep for the deep sorrow
carried by the strings. They mourn
life's passage, rising like notes from
Orpheus' lyre, his dirge of misery and loss,

of the certain death of looking back. Eurydice
forever sealed into the sulfureous grip of Hades.
Orpheus forever alone with his lifeless lyre,
his limp instrument of wailing, groaning, dying.

Cerberus howls through the hellish nights,
a refrain of vengeance and strife,
the paltry satisfactions of the underworld, ·
the shadow of life, the silence of the lyre.

"Adagio" echoes down cavern walls,
escaping into endless dark,
into the requiem for a love that lasts
only in the lovers' past, only in song.

Berries

1.

In the far corner of the grove,
night hurtles past the stars,
spews a black light to blank out
shadows. You say, "This is
the way the world ends.
Even the touch of lovers
does not last. It leads only
to an arousal we share
with the sheltering sky."

2.

I watch you clip berries to burnish
the jewels in your crown.
You count the spaces
left by hand-cut stones.
How hard they seem against
the crimson globes.
How pale when pressed
next to living flesh.
Eros hangs in the air
above low-lying limbs.
To grasp his desire means
another tree shall break
into blossom.

3.

I sense the joy as you
gather the rest of the harvest.
Heaps of stubble veil the view.
Leaves simmer
on orange embers,
nursing the flames
of nature's secret: *Nothing is lost,*
though everything wanders.

4.
You crush the berries
in a wooden bowl.
We stir the juices,
dip our fingers deep
into the swirl, write haiku
on each other's palms.
Night streaks by, shadows flee.
In the depths of darkness,
we feel the color of light:
O how our art will grow
to match the scale of our love.

The New Bathsheba

1.
She lingers before the bay window.
Birds flutter around her shadowed
face like butterflies drunk on nectar.
Her path looms, stony and steep,
tripping past orange canyon walls

and mountain streams fed by ferns.
Tiny pebbles mark her lane, strait
as the gate the blessed pass through.
A sheepfold looms on a sawback ridge.
Lambs murmur like captives in the desert.

She swoops her hand, and water springs up.
Her frown cuts channels through stagnant
ponds. Fishless, they succor dragonflies,
languid and long in diaphanous wings,
caressing the surface, landing with grace.

2.
How fitfully Hardy brings man and woman
together. Beauty lures but belies no truth.
Familiarity infuses false hope, seeds tragic
ends. Sheep roam, formless, lusting only
for food. Ahead, she packs away strands

of the sun. Night spreads like paint spilled
across the *atelier* floor, seeping into
divides of plank and nail. Her feet
skitter past the ovoid stain, kick up
sawdust to dapple the hue. It pales

in the floodlights of loves lost, loves
unredeemed by unity of spirit, unity
of touch, unity of laughter and pain.
Leaves layer like a rockless cairn.
Her touchstone weaves a mark of gold.

Luminous

1.
The light that cradles us
comes late to those who weep.
They wrap rays around them
like blankets of comfort:
illuminating the wounded heart,
shooing away dark tremors
of anxiety, stooping to flick
shadows from the cellars
of the self, sweeping sheaves
of *nada* outside the restless mind.

Brilliance descends in cosmic
crescendos. They resonate
as intimations of death's defeat.
The burial cave opens,
scrubbed clean of ungainly
defects, cloths neatly folded
on the cold slab of mortality.

2.
Knee-deep in tall grasses,
I watch the light ascend through
a chorus of mottled clouds.
I am ill prepared to accept this
inscrutable retreat, this rising
beyond all worldly difference.

Looking up, I stumble through
fallow fields, memory muffled
in astonishment. *What is* thrusts
into the light like a bull goring
a toreador, like X-rays bouncing off bone.

3.
I fold the light into origami shapes
of peace, each crease reinforced
by thumbnails, each piece
of radiance scored into recalcitrant joy.

Light baptizes living things with holy water,
mumbles, *In the name of the Father,*
of the Son . . . rushes through the sacrament,
retreats to a corner to recollect.

We live, move and have our being
in light. Yet we cannot pinpoint
its source without blinding ourselves.
The beneficent rays burn our retinas,
mining permanent darkness
from unending splendor.

4.
Light rules the kingdom
of ten thousand things. To be
banished from it means abiding
in our material form. This proves
insufferable. We, too, yearn to be
swept up in riches. We, too, reach
for the unseen god. We, too,
chase after the light.

Maxims

Under the aegis of the sun,
the adhesion of time peels
away in an amber glow.

This pagan dance of fatality
toils to oblivion in silence.
Ineffable, the senses cannot
bring us to Being.

The world escapes our actions.
Life becomes itself only as a pool
of yellow light spreads beneath
our feet. We wade in and thrive.

A curtain of salt descends
on the chosen few. They savor
it as a breath of wind flowing
across their brow.

In the cold purity of the sea,
no swimmer is recognized.

Patterns

The night sky replenishes itself
with a panoply of stars.
Dead, dying, each casts a glow
on the hungry world below.
Darkness shapes the diet
of its discordant inhabitants.

By day, they battle for a ray
of sun to illumine the face
of Narcissus within. Who
peers down on them with
feigned benevolence cracks
the mirror, wins approval of all.

Witnesses of the world's
turning tell of its crooked
descent. Epicurean atoms ping
like rain on the royal bedstead.
Behold how matter births
pleasure. Or so hedonists say.

Ecclesiastes declares it best:
Eat, drink and be merry, for we die.
Fast, thirst and sorrow: We also die.
Nuclei cohere only to burst apart.
Stars burn out, seep celestial shadows.
Millennia ahead, the world still turns.

Star Glow

branches brush against
the halo of heaven
limbs like long lithe
blades sharpen stone
angle through the dark

birds settle in treetops unseen
they exist only as they sing
a lilting lullaby to the drowsy
moon which turns its cratered
side toward a distant light

and sleeps through the notes
of the nocturne   fantasia
ballet of billowing ballasts
building up the anxious Earth
O how the rose of your lips

ignites my blood   how
the villanelle of your veins
wrests meaning from the void
writes variations on a theme
of absence and desire

a deconstructed desert landscape
blooms with floral flourishes
fertilized by shimmering stars
whose glow washes over the world
one half-veiled face at a time

Winter's Dawn

A screed of purple-red sky
breaks on the blank horizon.

Jewels cascade from clouds,
casting yellows across the Earth.

I homestead the desert, dredge
the depths of my hermit's cave.

No one dares follow or delve
into the blue well of solitude.

Serpents slither into the light,
slice through porous sand.

Arroyos barter for warmth
in the frisson of winter's dawn.

Snow settles on high mountains.
Crooked cacti slake my thirst.

I will make my final defense
beneath this dented dome.

Words shred on winnowing winds,
whisk away all trace of the wounded world.

I peer at their calligraphic scratches,
compose the poetry of the blind.

I am equal to all that endangers me,
even the cold, muted rays of the sun.

Beyond the Heat of Grains

1.
emerging from
shadowed kiva
ladder rises
piercing light

sandstone heat
heat of ruins
old world heat
heat of grains

elevation
height of heights

embers
glow to
blackened
charcoal

silent scrawl
waxing
warmth

dust
clouds
swirl

boot soles
skate
along
pink
floor

smooth
as gems
secret rites

2.
spirit dwells
above
commotion
shelling beans
water's weight

unhunted trail
path untrodden

scrubland
tangled
bush
of thorns

white cloud
sky
of blue
blue sky

noonday
heat
aching light

thirst
for meaning
hand-tied
rung

steps
toward
heaven
rocky
roof

of rock
and stars
level

wall
knife-edge
corner

reaching
high
to touch
cool
stone

overhead
ghostly
hand print

time's
embrace

beyond

Blue Guitar

(After Wallace Stevens)

The blue man with the blue guitar
no longer plays things as they are.

Things as they are are not so quick.
Blue men of substance aim, then kick

against the pricks of six-beat bars.
The bass line rumbles near and far.

Half-notes turn whole. Another hue
spews discord, then chords of blue

sprint beyond us as we are. And we
ourselves compose the tune in three-

quarter time. Harmony orbits a billion stars,
slingshots through our world of blue guitars.

Waiting for the Barbarians

(After Cavafy)

And so we wait
for the barbarians,
our hearts palpitating
like bleating sheep,
our mouths dry as stone,
our thirst unslaked
by the morning dew.

Beyond the ramparts,
the sun rises blood red
above the hill
where we hunted
for secrets of
the hordes to come.

We scattered high
and low, far past
the statue of Poseidon
that towers
at the edge of
the wine-dark sea,
which unfurls like
a murderous storm
that would drown our crops,
batter out battlements,
power the siege to come.

And so we wait
at the gates
for the barbarians
and the tsunami
that drives them on.

The Timeless Goal

(After Dante)

And so the dream begins
on the edge of a dark wood
without guide or companion,
no Virgil to mark my steps
deep into the netherworld of sin,
then upward, ever upward, beyond
all sense and sobriety to the celestial
sphere of perfection, paradise of the soul
that thirsts for living water, that stumbles
through the dark night toward its Source
of requited love, of illumination and
purgation and the splendor of the stars.

Their canopy spreads
over the breadth of my path
like a cloak on a winter's night, where
all is still, save the orbiting of the moon,
its high-frequency music cascading down
the spheres to where I wander in loneliness,
without guide or friend. O Virgil, when will
you come to me, as poet and muse? When
will you divide the branches of this wood,
through which I must pass toward union
with the divine, the embers of hell still
clinging to my feet, the heights of Purgatory
freshly scaled?
            Then Beatrice will relieve you
of your charge, the melancholy prologue
to my passage to my Beloved, as ethereal as
the thin night clouds, as substantial as my
living breath. She comforts and enlightens me,
guiding my steps ever higher toward my apotheosis

as the poet of the *Comedy*: the happy chance
of redemption and renewal, of release to the All in All.

The dark wood shines bright with the fire
of everlasting joy. Virgil, your cadences expand
through the spheres until I hear them march
beyond the bounds of creation. Their rhythms cling
to my feet, your lyrics imprint my light-filled soul
with the power of poetry that drives me
ever onward, nearer the mortal's timeless goal.

EVERLASTING
Book IV

OTHER SHORES

The Dark House of Death

Nobody is asleep on earth. Nobody, nobody.
— Federico Garcia Lorca, "City That Does Not Sleep"

Sporting white top hats, the Sierra Nevada mountains
butt up against the new dawn's Andalusian sky, casting
craggy shadows across the quiet *calles* of Granada.
Restlessly, the darkened city churns in its sleep.

Federico Garcia Lorca strums his yellow guitar,
tuning it to a *cante jondo*, a deep song of *duende*,
dark heart of flamenco and the bullfight and his own
fatalistic poems: moans of his inexorable execution

at Franco's hellish hands. Fascism fears the poet,
the ferocious oracle of *duende*, who rips out
the roots of authority, the dark clods of captivity,
who vows to dive underground, digesting bitter earth

like bullets from the firing squad. They shout, *Victoria!*
as Garcia Lorca's listless body slides along the bloodied
    wall.
Duende, he once told a lecture hall, haunts death's house.
It will not appear until it spies that fiercely angled roof.

* * *

In the branches of the laurel tree
I saw two dark doves
    — Federico Garcia Lorca, "Of the Dark Doves"

His mother bellows on the spirit's wind, over the hobbled
heads of the dead, in search of an inexpressible "new,"
the endless baptism of freshly created things, as Garcia Lorca
loved to lecture. Ending and refrain burn blood like glass.

Few mourners cast a spell over the public patrons gnawing
on his books, seeking some taste of destiny, identity, some
word of the eternal voice of Spain. I am no Spaniard,
yet I claim to be a poet. Garcia Lorca gifts me with his song.

Its maudlin melody marches up my spine, scorches
my eyes, which smolder under the noonday sun, spewing
ashes to ashes, igniting dust to dust. The dark memory
of the buried ruins of saddened Spain steadily seeps

through wilted wreaths tossed at Franco's feet. No
offering for the conqueror, they exude a sickly odor
of offal, of ordinary flesh rotting on shattered ribs.
Gunshot mixes with marrow, smoke fumigates the poem.

* * *

No one is sleeping in this world. No one, no one.
I have said it before.
     — Federico Garcia Lorca, "City That Does Not Sleep"

No one is sleeping, yet the world will not awaken.
The slain poet merits no notice. We bow our
heads in humiliation at the philistine ways
of savage, civilized societies. All cultural wealth

but poetry suffocates in its bed. *Duende* sends Garcia
Lorca's poems soaring above feeling and desire,
above the consecration of form. How many enjambments
mire in dark waters? How many stanzas lay bricks

of marble and salt? Garcia Lorca sings of hemlock and
demons, of Socrates and Descartes. But the profane
choruses of drunken sailors shatter any hope for his
new poetic style. They reject all the sweet geometry

that maps the darkened heart of southern Spain, where
Moors and Gypsies set up camp, pulling sleights of hand

on gullible gamblers, assured that Andalusia knows no
other artifice than the machine-gun-fire flights of flamenco.

* * *

In the branches of the laurel tree
I saw two naked doves
One was the other
and both were none
　　　— Federico Garcia Lorca, "Of the Dark Doves"

Garcia Lorca lies on the floor to fence with the phantoms
of his future. His black boots shine in the saddened sun.
The fattened face of Franco appears: an anxious cry for
more water, for dousing naked doves in *duende's* black pool.

Writers live and die like newly created roses. Aromas
rise from vast yearnings, inured to the penance of suffering.
Above *duende's* golden serpent, a crooked soldier salutes
the fruit of Fascism. Dawn's lemons dangle at the edge of
　　time.

Only 19 years embody Garcia Lorca's high-strung calling.
An awkward teen at his writing desk, he scribbles notes
about his mellifluous malaise. *Modernismo* flourishes in the
shadow songs of caves. Dark doves coo. *Duende* never lies.

His mother wails, wrapped in her mantilla of Spanish black
　　Head
thrown back, heels clicking hard, she swirls against the fiery
　　flanks
of flamenco. Prancing like an epic stallion, she nudges her
　　anguished
son: asleep, asleep. Today, *duende* has entered the dark house
　　of death.

Splendor

1.

Samuel Taylor Coleridge digests his grayish-green anodyne
and dreams of the kaleidoscopic exotica of Kublai Khan.

Orson Welles puffs his cigar between takes, edits and directs
the poet's smoke-thin visions into everlasting, silver celluloid.

Xanadu, palatial complex of Khan's magnificent Mongolian
    empire,
metamorphoses into the fantasy kingdom of Charles Foster Kane

and his flame-filled childhood. Fumes of sizzling rosebuds spew
traces of gray across his bejeweled grasping after operatic
    grandeur.

2.

Coleridge pens imagery of high-minded passion, tragic loss,
despair at sea — an epic Delacroix — while William Wordsworth

lets loose a clear-eyed revolution contra the high flowery stanzas
of England's prettified poetry. Plain diction and the depths

of the self, suckled by the mystic wonders of Lakeland's fells,
    attune
to the melody of the poet's maturation, nature's marvel of
    The Prelude.

Chubby, cherubic Coleridge chases after the lean, elegant
    Wordsworth
to connive an unpatched rupture in poetry's flow: birth of
    Romanticism.

3.

Kublai Khan's courtly poets conjure impossible imperial
    feats
to further the wise warrior mystique of China's first conqueror.

Grandson of Genghis Khan, he weaves the calligraphy of his
bravery into the broad shield he uses to rebuff temptation

of all but the serpentine lure of luxury and opulence, his rightful
reward, his cherished spoils, interest compounded daily at Xanadu.

A knock at the door, and Coleridge's dream tears asunder on film,
dissipating with the vapors rising from Welles' golden cigar.

4.
Wordsworth wanders lonely as a cloud, watchful of nature's glory
expressed in woodlands, mountains, and the steady wash of the sea.

This all can be praised without ornament, witnessed without
embellishment, an earthy channel for the radiance of the world

to bless us, even though the world is too much with us. How much
splendor can one soul gather into the barns of abundance?
      Coleridge,

dejected among his odes, seeks ever more film time. Khan, free
      of worldly
weariness, tallies his treasures. Wordsworth waves a daffodil
      and weeps.

Stone: A History

Osip Mandelstam writes his final poem
on stone. Other prisoners in the Soviet
gulag swing leaden sledgehammers
to crush rock. Every hundred pieces
equals one crust of bread. Pulverize
till you drop earns a damp pinch of salt
thrown over your shoulder.

Mandelstam's stomach rumbles. His empty
crime: mocking the great Stalin in verse,
manufacturing metaphors of cockroaches
lengthening the tyrant's mustache:
now a thick, furry barrier to free speech,
now a bristly edge of the black hole that
devours all hope, that ruins all rules of art.

Osip entertains Pasternak with his militant work.
Boris cries, "What you read . . . is not poetry,
it is suicide." Freezing in thin clothes in a
Siberian camp, Osip vows he will never bow
to the soulless rule of the Bolsheviks. His pen
will penetrate stone, he proclaims, sculpting
anti-symbolist verses as a monument to freedom.

On the icy steppes of Siberia, a political prisoner
named Dostoevsky begins *The House of the Dead*.
In it we read the tea leaves of Osip's destiny.
Shivering, emaciated, he volunteers to carry stones
to a construction site. His thin muscles aching, he
says, "My first book was called *The Stone*, and the stone will
be my last." He pitches a pinch of salt over his shoulder.

Others laugh as he gathers his poems in a rock pile
of remembrance. He succumbs to heart failure,
exhaustion. History faintly records that Stalin sucks

stones as he lies in state. The dust on his mustache spells, "Find, praise Osip." But as soon as he swallows, the letters vanish into the void, and the endless parade of lock-step pomp and circumstance begins.

Mists Before Dawn

Dull orange bracken clings to the peat-like soil that seeps
into muddy moors past Devon. A shadowy fog makes
a royal landing on the low-slung ridge, spewing
fists of mist fit for scalers of Lakeland mountains,
balancing on the knife edge of Helvellyn before dawn.

I follow the droppings-dappled sheep trails, veering away
from the road. A dirty white flock nuzzles the close-cropped
scrubland for shoots of greenery, but masticates only humid air.
In the dim light of evening, a dark presence looms on the uneven
horizon: a distinct world fitfully revealed and obscured, liberated
      from,
then confined to the clinging veil of illusion that clutches the
      Earth.

This is no pilgrimage into the noirish heart of nature,
yet I detect through the flattened corona of the monarch moon
outlines of a troupe of Shakespearean ghosts tottering my way.
Revealed and obscured, like questions in Hamlet's tragedy,
they would gladly chant as a Greek chorus, if only they had
material voices to be heard. Together, they mime the news

of Elizabethan England: betrayal and intrigue, executions
and sex. The lust for power pours the foundation of
the City of Man—sin and ambition, deception and pride. I hear
nothing but the constant scuff of my boots against wet stone.
Silence wraps round me like a cloak of quicksand. I must try
to scrape it clean. But with each new blade stroke, no novel
message emerges, no sign points homeward. Emptiness reigns
like a ruthless queen, virgin and shorn, an otherworldly white.

Looking back, I search for Coleridge strolling atop the
      Quantock Hills.
He has coaxed the Wordsworths there, convincing them to
      barter

isolation for inspiration. Poetry speaks to William, demanding
a new voice, a new style that joins the bright face of nature to
the brooding spirit of man, that lifts the lowly moments of the
    mundane
into the celestial heights of the poet's magisterial meditations on
    Being.

All this once would have sufficed for me, but the stale, soaked
    smell
of sheep reminds me that I remain alone. Night falls and the
    moors
glisten from the constant damp. No one comes to England for its
    weather or cuisine.
No one comes for solace or comfort or love. History, literature,
haute couture, base passions: Such is the recipe for a signal
    significance,
for a British extravagance of soul. It abides in the blackened
    bowels of Exmoor, launched from fallow footpaths
    and sodden goat trails,
skillfully trammeled by ghosts who juggle in silence the lavish
    jewels
of Elizabeth's crown, sparkling in the saturating mists before
    dawn.

Yorkshire

Ghosts peddle glory at the edge of the moors.
Poems materialize on shale. The Brontë sisters
dance a clumsy *pas de deux*, stumble down
steep stones to the dales.

The earth buckles yellow and green in great buckets
of paint that buoy gray bluffs protruding their brows.
They burst into the arrogant presence of time.
Rocks tumble, shape cairns with no arms.

Sunlight limns the empty lane I trod,
climbing through the infinite regress of fells.
They people the horizon in purples and blues,
stand guard, quell all tremors of fear.

A shadow, Charlotte haunts and rustles my steps,
like a sheep dog haranguing my pride.
Her intelligence, inventiveness, indomitable wit
overwhelm my slow, hesitant stride.

I am searching, for what I do not know, in the pages
of *Jane Eyre*. The scent of dark romance
marks a minor trail: Is "C. B." a woman or man? Yes.
And Yorkshire yearns to be the stuff of her dreams.

Bracken smothers all promise at the edge of the moors.
Poems scatter like spoors on the wind. Mushrooms
cling to the earth, mimic sediment and stone. No one
passes without usurping their throne.

The Brontës work a shadow magic to assuage the guilt,
calm the anxiety of their age. Betrayal, murder, illicit love.
These mar the woman who writes like a man. Yet Charlotte
would do no other. Her novels sprout like fault lines in shale.

The White Horse

1.
Chalk and silt cling to my boots as I skirt
the Uffington White Horse, a giant stallion
cast across the half-naked slope above me.

The horse whinnies when I ascend past its
sovereign flank, part of a 300-foot frame that bucks
and tumbles, paces and paws, in one direction.

I sense the majesty that fires this
expressionistic beauty, striving to outshine
the hubris of its hard-driven builders.

2.
On the upper angles of White Horse Hill,
deep trenches overflow with crushed, white
chalk, shaping the body of the ancient beast.

It is a feral creature, uncatchable, a great
white mystery, like Moby-Dick, the elusive
whale of Bronze Age artists.

The horse's hooves kick high to ward off
invaders. I climb farther toward its skinny head,
minus a mane, sleek as river rock.

3.
Alone in the approaching dusk, I stand unaided
as a pummeling wind powers past the crest
of the hill, coated in thin, thatched grasses.

I marvel at the mysticism of an image so
meticulously designed that it can be grasped
only from above, by the Anglo-Saxon gods.

But the White Horse is not meant to be seen.
It must be ridden. Now, Woden and Thunor cross
the deep, green vale. They need no bridle.

Fell Walking

1.
The spoor of spirit
spurs us on as we
amble in the flesh
through Grasmere's
glorious countryside.
The lakes liltingly
lure us to sigh along
their shimmering shores.
Here, England shines
with sustenance for
the sensitive soul.
The mystic marvels
at Cumbria's majestic
paths that lead beyond
the clutches of the mundane.
William Wordsworth
welcomed them: His poems
divulge the riddle of
existence, only to solve
it later on the fertile fells
and wondrous waters
of Lakeland.

2.
Sheep share their pastures
with weary walkers.
Fells echo our fears
of conquest and defeat.
We climb their patchwork
slopes and crest high
above the placid lakes,
high above the island
sprouting tall trees in
in the midst of Grasmere's

calm. Poetry permeates
the air; we breathe in
the diction of the common
man; we count the cost
of flouting the floral
ornamentation of Victorian
verse. No one calls this
high art anymore. Nature
defies decoration, deafens
the noisy diction of poets'
dandyish indulgences.

3.
Daffodils bloom beside
behemoth stone walls.
Clouds tonsure ridges
on the fells, towering
knife points of gray,
uneven stone. We
seek the serenity
of the lakes, their vellum
valleys and rocky alleyways
to Alcock Tarn. On my knees
I anxiously advance. Soon,
I slither to the summit.
An unhurried ascent.
Call it the Cumbrian crawl.
The Wordworths—
William and Dorothy—
wriggled their way to
the top. They planted
a golden pen and claimed
the land for art. No one
dares challenge their right.

Pink Rose

You clutch a dazzling pink rose
in front of the Spanish Steps.
The last of the day, bartered
for a block of chocolate.
No money changes hands.
No promises kept.
No way to go but headlong
into the crowds.
Tramping on tourists, staring past horses,
thinking Poesy inside the Keats House,
Piazza di Spagna 26.
Life mask, death mask.
Walls of poetical works bound
in shiny green leather.
Romanticism dies on the short, striped bed,
a sleigh ride to the Elysian Fields.
Awake to sweet unrest.
Here is my ode
to a rose not fading unto death.
No struggle for a breath.
Bright colors of the Steps
raise the bloom from Hades' depths.

Aria

Beauty affords no comfort
when you lie miles
away from the nearest *castello*,
where the owner serves
50-course dinners
for 50 euros apiece.
He hums Puccini
as he dishes the ravioli,
recommends strong red wine
from an earthy clay pitcher.

The white tablecloth drapes
my lap. I dare not stain it.
He is missing a button,
hits a high note, leaves
and returns.

Filled to unconsciousness,
we down the fiery *limoncello*.
Good for the digestion.
Good for scouring the esophagus.
Beside us a former
Olympic swimmer stabs
at her potatoes.
Her children stare down
from the staircase
with distorted faces,
inured to the feast,
imagining a beast
to torment.
Their potatoes grow cold.

A Puccini aria plays in my head.
Lucca, his hometown, looms
on the star-spewed horizon.
Even beauty is no match
for *la dolce vita*.

Lucca

Lying down
at the day's intermission,
I listen to Puccini arias,
and am transported to Lucca,
his walled hometown,
with its dirty-white streets,
its darkened straits,
its massive cathedral under
eternal construction.

Life limps along in
effervescent flux here,
beauty kept dormant,
or sprouting like a tree
from the *Torre Guinigi's*
grassy roof.

A one-time amphitheater
sports cloned tourist shops.
Only one
sells Puccini souvenirs.
La Boheme survives
on note cards, and
charts my tourist mood
of endless angst.

Opera is the grandest art,
some critics claim:
the human condition rendered
thick in symbol and sound.

Happily, I carry
the philosopher's stone
to decipher the soaring
scores.

They say, *passion, foreboding,*
no regrets. A fluttering
high C stirs the airwaves.
Ululating sopranos,
searing tenors sigh
heavenward.
The last act over,
the curtain rises on
the dull, restless, repetitive
routines of everyday life.

In the background,
echoes of *Tosca,* currents
of ruin and rust.
We must embrace our destiny
even on the off-notes.
Opera's solo signal:
Amor Fati.

Depths of Lucca

The only wisdom we can hope to acquire
is the wisdom of humility: humility is endless.
    —T. S. Eliot, *Four Quartets*

Chest-deep in the shadows
of the portico, I sip my champagne,
use a demitasse spoon to break
the crust of the flan. The flavor
floats on my tongue, evaporates
like dew. Memories linger for days.

Hip-deep in the sorrows
of reckless love, I smooth my shirt,
straighten my collar to shatter
the image of the maligned,
unkempt, no longer linked to the Other.
I stir my cold coffee, furrow into the past.

Knee-deep in the petty cares
of this world, I dig the grave for my riches,
toss clods of earth on the casket.
The aroma penetrates the hubris
of the poet, the humility of the wise.
From the magnolia tree, pink sweetness rises.

Las Meninas

I hurriedly push past myself,
watching my body from above,
feinting with consciousness,
fainting into the Spanish black.

Velazquez's *Las Meninas*
jack-hammers a tunnel
of *ek-stasis*, pulling me into
the painter's dark studio,

weighed down by overwhelming
curtains, curtailing the senses'
sense of majesty and control.
This is not *trompe l'oeil*. This is

tricking the soul into the artifice
of the palette, of paint on board,
of black that illumines perfect
placement: the spectator on the floor.

Stendhal's syndrome is no virtue
or vice. It suckles the sublime,
sated on illusion, art for art's sake,
delivering a blow to the solar plexus.

I gasp as my body trembles from tremors
of terror, annunciations of angels
bearing paintbrushes as paltry wings.
Their back feathers stained a Spanish black.

Painting owns no one, owes no one
comfort or joy or pedantic instruction.
The cherubs in the foreground radiate
innocence, wonder, humanity's blank heart.

At my feet, my body wriggles skyward,
wrenches for a transplant. Paint on it
Velazquez's black moustache, then part
the velvet curtains. I will rise to new life.

Tightrope

*You will never lack so much of the water of comfort that your
thirst will be intolerable.*
  — Teresa of Ávila, *The Way of Perfection*

Like the black-sheep sister of the Wallenda family,
St. Teresa totters on a tightrope hung high above
the ancient Roman aqueduct at Segovia. She searches
for a spigot to twist to quench the thirst for living waters
that mounts in the muddled masses below.

She has run away to the circus from the heavily walled
city of Ávila, its ramparts sprawling across the Castilian
plain. But there is no fortress fit enough to repel her
sacred charge. She knows that tightrope walking
thrills the crowds, while levitation, her supernatural-

born talent, stirs the mind, making mountains out of
miracles. We stare at her in amazement and yearn
to rise higher, homesick for the azure canopy of the sky,
for the peak experience of Transcendence with
a capital "T," trimmed down to one size fits all.

Tired travelers trickle in meandering streams toward
the Alcázar, an architectural sleight of hand, its 19th-
century, burned-out roofs meticulously reconstructed
decades later to resemble Disney's Magic Kingdom.
Behind, the U-shaped shadows of the aqueduct bend

low to embrace the Spanish black, the misery
of the unwitting hordes. Untutored, barely 20, Teresa
elevates above her convent's petty conflicts to an ecstasy
of divine love that quivers her Spanish self, emptied of all
save Bernini's marble statue of her that lies under scaffolding

in a tiny church in Rome. Flesh and bone, bread and wine
tighten their grip on her trailing leg. *Unloose me!*
she cries. And the angry clouds rip apart to let her
pass to the prime lookout point of the near-death
experiencer, peering down on her humble, impassioned life

as it edges into the rococo rooms of her interior
castle, looped by a languid moat that curries favor
only to fattened frogs, which she fears like demons.
A Doctor of the Church, Teresa lays her first-aid bag
gingerly on the tightrope, balancing the added weight

with the angle of her headpiece, coif, wimple and veil.
She gingerly pirouettes, miming an umbrella in hand.
Then she is not there, only the *shekinah* glory of God.
The crowd claps cautiously, wondering whether they
have paid too much. They bow, then lustily drink away.

The Lure of Portugal

The Duoro River floats lazily to the east,
the valley's hillsides splayed with vibrant vineyards.
Wine winnows the fruits of nature to a type of wisdom:
Grapes grab the dregs of the self, bathe the brain
in tides of *veritas*. Northern villages beckon.

In Nazare, fishermen scour the coast in search
of miraculous catches. They look for the Galilean
strolling the shore. Boats bob in the shallows.
Flaking paint dapples their colors: red, green, yellow.
Nets mended, the men wait for the sinking sun.

Lost on the back roads, I spy wizened widows
driving horse-drawn wagons on wobbly tires.
The intersection clogs with black scarves and frocks.
Farm work forms a sacrifice for their husbands' sins.
There is no other place to turn for solace. All is black.

Megalithic high-rises mar the view of Algarve's beaches.
Costa del Sol emigrates westward on the sun-drenched
sand. Tourists cling to their artificial paradise — exotic Iberia
with the comforts of home. A glass of Branco wine glints
in the sunset. No sound settles on the wings of Duoro wind.

Ode to Paris, 1986

Before the euro, you were—swirling light, sitting pretty.
We kicked it at night along the grungy lanes of *Ile de la Cité*.
Notre Dame loomed large and long, a battleship on the Seine.
An exoskeleton of Gothic bones, what could it do but win?

Hunger hung out among us, an unwanted dog on a wayward
    walk.
Frenchmen directed us *au centre*. In those days, I could talk the talk.
Still can, still do, but who needs "*J'adore vos diamants de luxe,
calme et beauté*" when you must bow down in a row sans your
    ducks?

Serendipity, man, that's what *la Cité* seeped. Evening, an ermine
blanket tossed effortlessly over the spires of the medieval vermin
that Haussmann hacked into Euclidean lines of parallel charms:
more *ordre, beauté et calme*. Organic geometry. What's the harm?

Dusk draped us in *l'amour du mystère*. Cafe awnings as exotic
as Flaubert's Egyptian tours, plump with mistresses for the neurotic
novelist who poisoned Normandy with naturalistic despair. He's
no Parisian, no architect, no monk. We absorb *le mot juste*; a star
    flees.

On the sidewalk, a 50-franc note calls out beneath the weeds.
We look for an owner, see nothing, feel nothing but the need to
    feed
on crepes, *chocolat et confiture de fraise*. I imagine Camus and Sartre
at *Les Deux Magots*, nursing black *café*, pouring *noir* into your heart.

Plague Year

The genome tilts on its axis, spilling memes of shame,
mutation and death, tattooed on plasma walls.

Coronavirus latches onto a lowly cell, clamps down,
spews pellets of bubonic plague as fleas flee disaster.

1666. Eyam Village barricades its boundaries: *No going in.*
No going out. The population dies like convulsing rats,

bodies stacked high in the street: cords of firewood. No one dares
light the flame. Pestilence obeys the border's blockade, contained

behind thick, golden stones. Tiny cottages transform to infirmaries.
Judgment seeps through window panes. Mercy aligns with death.

We build no blockades; boundaries shift in the wind. Virus
     obeys
no one's laws, vandalizes the body, sets fire to human touch.

Eyam beams prettiness now. Neat, manicured lawns, well
     swept streets,
no trace of plague save on the village entry sign. Tourists flock
     like fleas,

soaking up history's survival, sobering on its showcase of blight.
Who deserves to die from nature's aberrations? *Who goes in,*
     who out?

Bones

I sit cross-legged in the darkness
of my cave of solitude.
I have fought hard
for this lonely life.
To any who come after,
my scattered bones
will be a fiery treasure.

About the Author

Arlice W. Davenport

is the author of *Setting the Waves on Fire* (Meadowlark Press, 2020). He has been writing poems for more than fifty years, first spurred on after reading E. E. Cummings in a high school English class. Cummings' diction was kinetic; his use of language innovative and spry, springing from a deep need for vitality and creative freedom that could effortlessly twist punctuation, syntax and spacing into new, barely recognizable forms.

Early on, Davenport understood Cummings' radical, Dadaist poems as primarily surface play across the page. Now, he realizes that Cummings was searching for the primal language beyond modern American English, for the Ur-metaphor "This is that," the mystical energy of his poetic art.

Today, Davenport aims at that same type of mystic poetry, after having had an epiphany in his twenties in the archaeological villa near Chichen Itza in Yucatan, Mexico.

In the prose poem "Awakening," he expresses the strength and lasting impact of that epiphany:

The sky wavered orange and gray, as dusk settled over the Mayan ruins, the Yucatan scrubland, the cooling tiles of the archaeological villa outside Chichen Itza, where we stayed. I sat poolside, contemplating the fading, fiery orb of the sun, musing on Kukulcan, the sacred cenote, the Mayans' murderous ball game, their majestic pyramid, and rows upon rows of chiseled skulls. When suddenly an epiphany engulfed me: I saw my life come together as a perfect whole, from beginning to end, and it showed one thing only: that I would be and remain a writer. My soul rose in ecstasy. I have never failed to feed it since.

Davenport, a lifelong Wichitan, is the retired Travel editor and Books page editor for *The Wichita Eagle* newspaper. With his wife, Laura, he has explored Europe more than thirty times. They are still in awe of the journey.

Acknowledgments

This book, the debut of Meadowlark Poetry Press, would not have been possible without the expert aid of the following people.

Tracy Million Simmons, publisher extraordinaire of Meadowlark Books, believed in and nurtured the publication of this book from the start. Her patience, guidance and keen professional interest turned an inchoate idea into the completed text you hold in your hands. She inspires, nurtures and gently prompts until the poet thinks her ideas are his own. Thank you, Tracy. Working with you was a pleasure and a victory.

Linzi Garcia, Meadowlark publicist, assiduously designed the interior of this book and edited my first woolly manuscript into shape. Her enthusiasm and willingness to tolerate my obsessive corrections and changes of plan smoothed the way to this beautiful book, which expresses my desire to create a visual and written work of art. She brought an organizational eye and artistic sensibility to the exacting task.

Laura Davenport, my wife, not only put up with my endless revisions and hours on the computer trying to find *le mot juste* for each line of every poem, but she lent her considerable knowledge and talent to helping me design the cover of the book. Placement and choice of typography were hers. And she encouraged my treatment of the celestial cover photo. As always, I send her all my love.

Finally, my great friend **Norman Carr** spurred my pursuit of excellence by his meticulous abstract paintings illustrating poems from my first book, *Setting the Waves on Fire* (Meadowlark, 2020). He uncovered the potential of every new poem, and his paintings showed how that potential could be realized in more than one medium. I am deeply in his debt.

Meadowlark

Poetry
Press

Emporia, Kansas USA

www.ingramcontent.com/pod-product-compliance
Lightning Source LLC
Chambersburg PA
CBHW020918090426
42736CB00008B/687